MILITARY VEHICLES

U.S.
NAVY
DESTROYERS

by Martha E. H. Rustad

Reading Consultant:
Barbara J. Fox
Reading Specialist
North Carolina State University

Capstone

Mankato, Minnesota

Blazers is published by Capstone Press,
151 Good Counsel Drive, P.O. Box 669, Mankato, Minnesota 56002.
www.capstonepress.com

Library of Congress Cataloging-in-Publication Data
Rustad, Martha E. H. (Martha Elizabeth Hillman), 1975–
  U.S. Navy destroyers / by Martha E. H. Rustad.
    p. cm.—(Blazers. Military vehicles)
  Summary: "Describes U.S. Navy Destroyers, including their design,
equipment, weapons, crew, and missions"—Provided by publisher.
  Includes bibliographical references and index.
  ISBN-13: 978-0-7368-6460-2 (hardcover)
  ISBN-10: 0-7368-6460-1 (hardcover)
  1. Destroyers (Warships)—United States—Juvenile literature.
I. Title. II. Series.
V825.3.R88 2007
623.825'40973—dc22   2006000520

Editorial Credits
Amber Bannerman, editor; Thomas Emery, set designer; Ted Williams, designer;
    Jo Miller, photo researcher/photo editor

Photo Credits
Check Six/Dan Megna, 26–27; Tom Twomey, 6
Corbis Sygma, 13 (top)
DVIC/PH2 Felix Garza, 24; PH2 James Elliott, cover
Photo by Ted Carlson/Fotodynamics, 10–11, 20–21, 28–29
U.S. Navy Photo, 17; PHAA Ronald A. Dallatorre, 25 (top); PHAN Eben
    Boothby, 7; PHAN Marvin E. Thompson Jr., 16; PH1 Michael W.
    Pendergrass, 4–5; PH1 Shane T. McCoy, 14–15; PH2 James Elliott, 8–9;
    PH2 Phillip A. Nickerson Jr., 22–23; PH2 Rebecca Kearns, 13 (bottom);
    PH3 Joshua Word, 25 (bottom); PH3 Randall Damm, 18–19

**Capstone Press thanks Rear Admiral Steven G. Smith, United States Navy
    (Retired), for his assistance in preparing this book.**

1 2 3 4 5 6 11 10 09 08 07 06

TABLE OF CONTENTS

DESTROYERS

Day after day, U.S. Navy destroyers glide quietly through the ocean waves. Their powerful radar and sonar systems search for enemy ships, planes, and submarines.

BATTLE GROUP

Since 1901, fast destroyers have been in battles at sea. Destroyers protect other U.S. Navy ships in battle groups.

DESIGN

A destroyer has a steel frame, or hull. A tall superstructure rises from the deck of the ship. The crew controls the ship from a room in the superstructure.

SUPERSTRUCTURE

A destroyer avoids being attacked by moving quietly through the water. Their engines can become quieter to avoid being detected by enemy submarines.

BLAZER FACT

Destroyer engines can produce up to 100,000 horsepower. The average car produces 160 horsepower.

Destroyers are built to stay safe in enemy attacks. They also have powerful weapons to defend themselves in battles.

BLAZER FACT

In an attack in 2000, enemies blew a large hole in the side of destroyer USS *Cole*. The U.S. Navy repaired the ship and began to use it again in 2003.

USS COLE

WEAPONS AND EQUIPMENT

Radar and sonar systems on destroyers search for possible threats. The systems scan the air and sea to find enemy planes, ships, and submarines.

15

The radar system can even find
enemy missiles flying through the air.
Destroyers then use their own missiles to
blast enemy missiles out of the sky. Other
destroyer missiles attack targets on land.

Helicopters take off from and land on the deck of a destroyer. The helicopters carry torpedoes, missiles, and guns.

BLAZER FACT

Some destroyers can store helicopters in an onboard hangar.

USS JOHN PAUL JONES

RADIO ANTENNAS

GUN

MISSILE LAUNCHER

RADAR

LANDING DECK

SUPERSTRUCTURE

OUT TO SEA

As many as 380 sailors work on a destroyer. Their jobs vary from steering the ship to cooking meals.

Some sailors help keep the ship running smoothly. They load weapons. Others draw charts and run equipment.

Destroyers work hard to find enemy targets and defend against attacks. The U.S. Navy depends on destroyers to keep the oceans safe for America.

BLAZER FACT

The U.S. Navy spends about $20 million each year to run each destroyer.

WATCHING THE SEA!

JOHN PAUL JONES

29

GLOSSARY

hull (HUHL)—the frame or body of a ship

missile (MISS-uhl)—an explosive weapon that can travel long distances

radar (RAY-dar)—equipment that uses radio waves to find and guide objects

sonar (SOH-nar)—equipment that uses sound waves to find underwater objects

submarine (SUHB-muh-reen)—a ship that can travel both on the surface of and under the water

superstructure (SOO-per-struhk-chur)—the part of a ship that rises above the main deck

torpedo (tor-PEE-doh)—a missile that travels underwater

READ MORE

Doeden, Matt. *The U.S. Navy*. Blazers: The U.S. Armed Forces. Mankato, Minn.: Capstone Press, 2005.

Stone, Lynn M. *Destroyers*. Fighting Forces on the Sea. Vero Beach, Fla.: Rourke, 2005.

Streissguth, Thomas. *The U.S. Navy*. U.S. Armed Forces. Minneapolis: Lerner, 2005.

INTERNET SITES

FactHound offers a safe, fun way to find Internet sites related to this book. All of the sites on FactHound have been researched by our staff.

Here's how:
1. Visit *www.facthound.com*
2. Choose your grade level.
3. Type in this book ID **0736864601** for age-appropriate sites. You may also browse subjects by clicking on letters, or by clicking on pictures and words.
4. Click on the **Fetch It** button.
FactHound will fetch the best sites for you!

INDEX